P9-AOA-716

*"When I was young, my ambition was to be
one of the people who made a difference in this world."*
—Jim Henson (1936–1990)

jim HENSON
The Guy Who Played with Puppets

By Kathleen Krull

Paintings by
Steve Johnson and Lou Fancher

RANDOM HOUSE 🏠 NEW YORK

Jim Henson's family didn't have a TV. No one had a TV in the 1930s.

So how could a lively boy entertain himself? By kicking off his shoes and loving his life along the Mississippi River.

A creek bubbled right past Jim's big old farmhouse. That's where he and his brother, Paul, fished and swam. On hot, humid nights, they watched fireflies flickering and listened to frogs croaking nonstop in the swamps. Listening, watching, singing, and telling stories—that was entertainment.

Daydreaming and nature watching kept him busy, observing the animals and birds of Leland, Mississippi. He took care of his pets—his dog, Toby, his pony, turtles, snakes, frogs. He drew what he saw and also what he imagined—filling notebooks with creatures he made up.

At his grandparents' house, he liked to listen to his cousins trying to top each other with hilarious stories at the dinner table.

He was closer to his grandmother than to anyone else in his family. For hours, they would sit on the porch, rocking back and forth, as she stitched beautiful quilts or painted, or told him stories—and, most important, listened to his.

Usually he kept his thoughts to himself. He didn't like to bother people.

With friends, including a best friend named Kermit, he played games. Not team sports (he was always the last to be chosen). But Ping-Pong and tennis and board games.

He put on shows for the family in the backyard, using props he found around the house. A sheet and towel from his mother's linen closet? Perfect as a cloak and turban while he played a flute to cast a spell on the coiled garden hose, posing as a snake.

He made his first public appearance as a Cub Scout. While a fellow Scout tried to tell jokes, Jim stood behind him, wrapped his arms around his friend's chest, and waved a white handkerchief in his face. Everyone giggled. Making people laugh—to Jim, that was magic.

In search of more, he performed in school plays, working behind stage as well.

Still no TV, but he and Paul built their own crystal radio set. Jim hurried home from school to catch action shows like *The Green Hornet* and *The Shadow.* On Sunday nights, he loved a comedy with ventriloquist Edgar Bergen talking to his "dummy," a wooden puppet named Charlie McCarthy.

Comic strips and books fed his imagination. He was especially impressed with the way L. Frank Baum created a world alive with details in the Oz series.

He wrote poetry, and he kept drawing, illustrating every school report whether the teachers asked him to or not.

Saturday afternoons were for going to the movies. The first one he ever saw was MGM's *The Wizard of Oz.* It remained his favorite—once he got over being scared by the lion's roar that started every movie from MGM.

Jim's thirteenth year stood out. A daily newspaper published one of his cartoons—his first appearance in print.

By now, his family was living in Hyattsville, Maryland. TV sets were showing up in some homes, and Jim nagged his parents nonstop to buy one.

They resisted, worrying that TV was a bad influence on children. But in 1950, they gave in.

The set was small, with fuzzy images in black and white. But TV connected people—like his family, as they gathered in the living room to watch shows together, shows that were actually being filmed *somewhere else*. Magic! He liked many programs, especially a puppet show called *Kukla, Fran, and Ollie.* It starred a group of cloth puppets called the Kuklapolitan Players, and it made his whole family laugh.

His father, a biologist, wanted Jim to prepare for a career in science.

Too late. Within a few years, Jim was looking for a TV job. Playing with puppets seemed a promising idea.

Puppets struck some people as babyish, but Jim really wanted to go on TV. Now! He checked out books from the library and joined his high school's puppet club as a way to learn how to make them.

One day, he saw an ad. A Saturday-morning show needed young people to work with marionettes, working the strings of these traditional puppets. Jim and a friend built Pierre the French Rat, plus two cowboy puppets, Longhorn and Shorthorn, and answered the ad.

They got the job. At sixteen, Jim was on TV, playing with puppets.

His father was sure puppets could not provide a proper career. So in college, Jim tried taking science courses. But art classes won out—they were so much more fun, even if they were often in the home economics department. He was one of six men amid five hundred future wives and mothers majoring in home ec, with its classes in puppetry, costume design, and advertising art.

While still in college, Jim got his very own TV show—*Sam and Friends.* Hosted by a bald puppet named Sam, this five-minute puppet comedy ran twice a day on a Washington, D.C., channel.

Jim wanted his creatures to be able to smile or frown or express any emotion. So instead of wood, he used flexible, furry fabrics to make Mushmellon, Icky Gunk, and the others. For Sam's friend Kermit, he cut up his mom's old green cloth coat and stitched it into a funny shape. Then he stuck on eyes made from a Ping-Pong ball he'd cut in half. He liked to make eyeballs slightly crossed, for a funnier look.

He practiced for hours in front of a mirror, trying to get his puppets' movements and expressions just right, voicing silly and witty thoughts he normally kept to himself.

He got rid of the usual boxy stage for puppets—the TV screen was now the stage. That meant squatting below the camera's range and holding puppets over his head, getting sore arms from keeping them in action. Taking advantage of the new technology of color TV, he filled sets with vivid hues.

Jim asked Jane Nebel, a woman from his puppetry class, to help out. They started calling their creations Muppets—just a fun word to say, sort of a combination of "marionettes" and "puppets."

Sam and Friends ran for six successful years. Those who worked with Jim were impressed:

"The kid is positively a genius."

"A phenomenon . . . with everyone from kids to great-grandmothers."

"We had never seen *anything* like that before."

Jim drove to his college graduation in a secondhand Rolls-Royce that he'd bought himself—and received his degree from the home economics department.

Still—a grown man playing with puppets? Even Jim had his doubts.

He sailed off to Europe to paint. In his free time, he went to puppet shows and met famous puppeteers proud to be working in what was considered a serious art form there. He learned that for centuries people all over the world had used puppets for ceremonies, entertainment, debate, and much more.

Returning to the United States, Jim no longer felt puppets were childish. He formed a company called Muppets, Inc. And he married Jane.

All during the 1960s, the Hensons' Muppets made watching TV commercials fun—they starred in hundreds of commercials, selling everything from detergent to dog food. Jim and Muppets like Kermit started making audiences laugh with their guest appearances on popular TV programs like *The Ed Sullivan Show.*

At the same time, Jim experimented with other ways of letting his imagination soar, such as making films. Some projects worked, some didn't, but a failure never stopped him from trying something new.

His moments of inspiration came when he was relaxing outside or on a comfy chair in his office. He never forgot being under a certain tree in California, awestruck at the beauty in nature, leaves flickering in the sun. On whatever paper was handy, he would take his favorite bright-colored felt-tip pens and begin sketching.

Fifteen years after introducing the Muppets, Jim was thirty-three and a famous guy on TV.

One day in 1968, he got a phone call that would change his life. It was from a TV producer named Joan Ganz Cooney. She told him about studies showing the vast difference that preschool education made in children's lives. Poor children usually had no access to it—but they did have TVs. Could TV be used to *teach*? And would his Muppet company help her new show for preschoolers?

Jim hesitated. The show had a weird name—*Sesame Street.* Joan explained that just as the command "Open Sesame" in the old Arabian tale opened a door to treasure, she wanted her show to open doors in young minds. Jim wasn't sure he wanted to limit his Muppets to children.

But years of watching his own children convinced him. He'd always studied them, figuring out what made them laugh, listening to their stories, encouraging their imaginations. Maybe TV *could* be a good influence. During a frightening time when some felt the country was falling apart, maybe this could be his contribution, to help change it for the better.

At least he'd be the fun guy, the one who made sure the show, for all its noble goals, didn't get too preachy. Plus it was a big experiment. Jim *loved* to experiment.

Along with a team of brilliant writers and musicians at Joan's new Children's Television Workshop, Jim's company got busy.

Kermit the Frog was ready to go. Soon came a crabby creature who lived in a garbage can—Oscar the Grouch. Then two quite different friends named Bert and Ernie. A hungry guy named Cookie Monster. A really big bird named Big Bird. And many more.

Jim worked hard, sketching each new Muppet in the brightest of colors, then guiding its creation. He was the spark behind each Muppet's personality and voice, which made learning—letters, numbers, all sorts of concepts—weirdly appealing.

Working with all the other creative people, he spoke so softly that they had to lean in to hear him. He would burst out laughing at their clever ideas or say "Hmm" if he saw room for improvement. "Lovely!" was his highest compliment. Or else he'd murmur, "I think it could be funnier."

Sesame Street launched on November 10, 1969. Jim zoomed around the set, getting this ultimate puppet show ready to go. He was the high-pitched voice of Ernie and Kermit and other Muppets, and he contributed short animated films he'd produced for the show. He even made a rare appearance as himself, juggling three balls in a counting skit.

"Three balls" was his line.

This show was unique—using laughter to help preschool children learn, and never talking down to them. Everyone used words like "noble," "exciting," and "revolutionary" to describe it.

Bert, Ernie, and the others soon became best friends to millions of children around the world getting ready for school.

Sesame Street went on to win many awards and become the most influential and longest-running children's program in history. Jim's Muppets were vital to the show's success, inspiring witty dialogue and hilarious stories. They were a lot like real kids: cute, cuddly, giddy, greedy, grinning, not perfect or sweet. They were just so much *fun.*

Jim's own five children—Lisa, Cheryl, Brian, John, and Heather—kept inspiring him and went on to help the show in various ways.

Traveling between his six homes, with many more plans up his sleeve, Jim supervised movie and TV projects that used other ways of playing with puppets.

Muppets helped introduce the first season of *Saturday Night Live* in 1975, and then starred in their own show the following year. *The Muppet Show*—with Kermit, Miss Piggy, and eventually some four hundred others—was for all ages. It was Jim's dream to create a show for the whole family—the kind of entertainment he would have loved with his family back in Mississippi. The Muppets became the most popular puppets in the history of the world, coaxing giggles from as many as 235 million people each week.

Jim went on to make several hit Muppet movies and also worked on other people's projects. He helped with the creation of Jedi Master Yoda in *Star Wars: The Empire Strikes Back,* for example, and assisted with the creatures in the Teenage Mutant Ninja Turtles movies. And he kept making experimental films with his own puppets, but not the adorable Muppets. Not everyone loved those serious movies like *The Dark Crystal* or *Labyrinth* at first, but his experiments seemed endless.

It was heartbreaking to everyone who knew him—and to millions who didn't—when Jim Henson died unexpectedly, after a short illness, at the age of fifty-three.

Thousands came to his memorial service. As he had wished, everyone wore bright colors, and a jazz band from New Orleans played lively tunes.

At the end, people waved butterfly puppets of every hue, celebrating him and his work. With his vivid imagination—and playful way with puppets—Jim Henson had made a difference in this world.

SOURCES

*(*especially for young readers)*

BOOKS

Davis, Michael. *Street Gang: The Complete History of* Sesame Street. New York: Viking, 2008.

* Durrett, Deanne. *Jim Henson.* San Diego: KidHaven, 2002.

Finch, Christopher. *Jim Henson: The Works—The Art, the Magic, the Imagination.* New York: Random House, 1993.

* Gikow, Louise. *Meet Jim Henson: The Creative Mind Behind the Muppets.* New York: Random House, 1993.

Gikow, Louise. Sesame Street: *A Celebration—40 Years of Life on the Street.* New York: Black Dog & Leventhal, 2009.

Henson, Jim. *It's Not Easy Being Green, and Other Things to Consider.* New York: Hyperion, 2005.

Inches, Alison. *Jim Henson's Designs and Doodles: A Muppet Sketchbook.* New York: Abrams, 2001.

Morrow, Robert W. Sesame Street *and the Reform of Children's Television.* Baltimore: Johns Hopkins University Press, 2006.

* Parish, James Robert. *Jim Henson: Puppeteer and Filmmaker.* New York: Ferguson, 2006.

WEBSITES

Center for Puppetry Arts, puppet.org

The Jim Henson Foundation (promoting contemporary American puppet theater), hensonfoundation.org

The Jim Henson Legacy, jimhensonlegacy.org

Jim Henson's Creature Shop, creatureshop.com

Muppet Central, muppetcentral.com

Muppet Wiki, muppet.wikia.com

Puppeteers of America, puppeteers.org

* *Sesame Street,* pbskids.org/sesame

Sesame Workshop, sesameworkshop.org

YouTube, search results for "Jim Henson" and "commercials" (for pre–*Sesame Street* work)

To the always playful Dalia Hartman Bergsagel and Robin Hansen,
and in memory of Janet Schulman, a joy to work with
—K.K.

For Janet Schulman, with deepest gratitude
—S.J. and L.F.

Text copyright © 2011 by Kathleen Krull
Jacket art and interior illustrations copyright © 2011 by Steve Johnson and Lou Fancher

Photograph of Jim Henson courtesy of The Jim Henson Company.

Visit us on the Web! www.randomhouse.com/kids

Educators and librarians, for a variety of teaching tools, visit us at www.randomhouse.com/teachers

Library of Congress Cataloging-in-Publication Data
Krull, Kathleen.
Jim Henson : the guy who played with puppets / by Kathleen Krull ; illustrated by Steve Johnson and Lou Fancher. — 1st ed.
 p. cm.
ISBN 978-0-375-85721-8 (trade) — ISBN 978-0-375-95721-5 (lib. bdg.) — ISBN 978-0-375-98914-8 (ebook)
1. Henson, Jim—Juvenile literature. 2. Puppeteers—United States—Biography—Juvenile literature. 3. Television producers and directors—United States—Biography—Juvenile literature. 4. Muppet show (Television program)—Juvenile literature.
I. Johnson, Steve, ill. II. Fancher, Lou, ill. III. Title.
PN1982.H46K78 2011 791.5'3092—dc22 [B] 2010043837

MANUFACTURED IN CHINA   10 9 8 7 6 5 4 3 2 1   First Edition